WHEN PLANTS ATTACK

STRANGE AND TERRIFYING PLANTS

REBECCA E. HIRSCH

M Millbrook Press • Minneapolis

Dedicated to those working to study and protect the plants of the world

Millbrook Press
A division of Lerner Publishing Group, Inc.
241 First Avenue North
Minneapolis, MN 55401 USA

For reading levels and more information, look up this title at www.lernerbooks.com.

Main body text set in Caecilia LT Std 11/16.
Typeface provided by Adobe Systems.

Library of Congress Cataloging-in-Publication Data

Names: Hirsch, Rebecca E., author.
Title: When plants attack : strange and terrifying plants / Rebecca E. Hirsch.
Description: Minneapolis : Millbrook Press, [2019] | Audience: Age 9–14. | Audience: Grade 4 to 6. | Includes bibliographical references and index.
Identifiers: LCCN 2018022633 (print) | LCCN 2018024717 (ebook) | ISBN 9781541543881 (eb pdf) | ISBN 9781541526709 (lb : alk. paper)
Subjects: LCSH: Poisonous plants—Juvenile literature. | Dangerous plants—Juvenile literature.
Classification: LCC QK100.A1 (ebook) | LCC QK100.A1 H57 2019 (print) | DDC 581.6/59—dc23

LC record available at https://lccn.loc.gov/2018022633

Manufactured in the United States of America
1-44611-35514-8/13/2018

CONTENTS

INTRODUCTION

BEWARE THE KILLER PLANTS!

In 1581 an explorer warned of an island in the South Pacific, known only as the Island of Death. On this island grew the Death Flower. The large, beautiful flower formed a cave that a person could enter. Once inside, the flower's strange perfume lulled its visitor to sleep. Then the flower folded its petals tight and devoured the sleeping victim.

Over the years, other explorers told tales of deadly plants they had encountered. A naturalist named Dunstan relayed the terrifying story of a vampire vine in Nicaragua. While Dunstan and his dog were exploring a swamp, the dog let out a high-pitched squeal, and Dunstan found the animal wrapped in ropelike vines. The dog struggled and whined, as if in great pain. Dunstan hacked at the vine with his knife and, with great difficulty, freed the animal. To his horror, as he sliced at the vines, they curled around his arms like living fingers and left his skin red and blistered.

Does the idea of killer plants send a chill down your spine? If so, you're not alone. These plants make for thrilling tales, but you might not want them growing in your neighborhood.

An image of a murderous tree from Sea and Land by J. W. Buel. The 1889 book told fantastic tales of blood-thirsty plants and other "wonderful and curious things of nature."

Fortunately, the plants in these old explorer's tales aren't real. Scientists know beyond a doubt: flowers don't devour people. Vampire vines don't attack and strangle dogs.

But are there flowers that lure animals for their own dark purposes? Vines that suck the juices from their fellow creatures? Plants that cause terrible pain or even death? Definitely.

Plants can be murderers, kidnappers, or just monstrously misbehaved.

Come take a walk on the dark side of the plant world. But tread carefully. It's a jungle out there.

CHAPTER 1

STINGING TREE

Picture this: You are walking along a trail through a rain forest in Australia. There, beside the path, sits a shrub covered with huge, fuzzy leaves. The leaves look so velvety soft that you want to touch one. You reach out your hand.

Stop!

Don't let the plant's harmless appearance fool you. This is the stinging tree, also known as the gympie. It is the most painful plant in the world. It attacks anyone who touches it with sharp, poison-filled hairs.

One touch and you'll feel as if you've been stung by angry hornets. Your heart will race. You'll begin dripping with sweat. Your joints will swell and throb.

Dogs, horses, and even people have died after a brush with the stinging tree. A soldier reportedly shot himself after using a stinging tree leaf as toilet paper. Another soldier who fell into the plant during military training in 1941 had to be tied down to a hospital bed *for three weeks* because the pain was so bad. The pain can take years to go away completely.

Such a tiny mistake. Such a horrible punishment.

THE MYSTERY OF THE GYMPIE'S STING

In the wild, every plant is at risk of being eaten. Plants can't run away, so they must defend themselves. To do so, they may wield sharp thorns, ooze a sticky gum, or fill their leaves with bitter poisons.

But the stinging tree takes self-defense to a horrifying level. Even though it is called a tree, it's really a big shrub that grows in clearings in the Australian rain forest. How painful is its sting? Just ask Marina Hurley.

"Being stung is the worst kind of pain you can imagine—like being burnt with hot acid and electrocuted at the same time," said Hurley, an ecologist who has studied what eats the tree.

Stinging hairs cover every inch of the plant from the ground up—stems, fruits, and leaves. The sharp hairs are made of silica—the same substance found in glass—and are filled with poison. They break off with the slightest touch and jab into the skin like poison-filled needles. If the skin closes over the tiny hairs, the pain can come back years later. A hot shower, a cold shower, or a touch of the stung area—and the pain returns.

ATTACKER: *Dendrocnide moroides*

ALIASES: stinging tree, stinging bush, gympie, gympie stinger, suicide plant

ATTACK STRATEGY: stings animals and people with poison-filled hairs

KNOWN WHEREABOUTS: sunny clearings in the rain forest of northeastern Australia

The fuzzy leaves of the stinging tree are covered with poisonous hairs. One touch can mean months of pain.

The identity of the poison is a mystery. One researcher actually purified the poison and—foolishly—injected it into himself. He suffered horribly. But he did prove that the poison, and not the sharp hairs, cause most of the pain.

What's more, you can suffer just from breathing near a stinging tree. The plant sheds stinging hairs into the air. Those hairs can cause an allergic reaction or a nosebleed. Hurley's first encounter hurled her into a sneezing fit. Her eyes and nose ran for hours.

Hurley eventually figured out how to work near such a dangerous tree. She strapped on a surgical mask to breathe safely, and she pulled on thick welding gloves to handle the leaves. Still, she was stung at least ten times. Her worst sting came when she dropped her glove on the ground. "As I picked it up, I drove my finger right through a dead leaf that was curled up on the

Hollow silica hairs are filled with a powerful poison. The identity of the poison is a mystery.

forest floor," she said. She had to spend the rest of the day in the hospital.

So this tree must have the best defense ever against being eaten, right? Actually, no!

Hurley said the plant is crawling with spiders, beetles, ants, snails, frogs, and lizards. Shiny blackish-green beetles munch the leaves, avoiding the hairs. Rain forest birds gobble the bright pink fruits whole. A rain forest kangaroo—called the red-legged pademelon (PAH-dee-meh-lon)—can strip all the leaves off the plant in a single night.

Hurley said that many rain forest animals are either immune to the poison or can tolerate an awful lot of pain. "Obviously [the poison is] not working for a lot of animals."

So what is the point of the stinging tree's sting? One expert says that the stinging tree's poison may have been

To study what eats the stinging tree, Marina Hurley had to venture into the rain forest at night—and dress as if going into battle.

for Diprotodonts, enormous wombatlike creatures that are now extinct. These 3-ton (2.7 t) herbivores used to rumble through the rain forests of Australia, scarfing down as much as 330 pounds (150 kg) of vegetation a day. The giants disappeared about twenty-five thousand years ago. Maybe the poison is a weapon against an enemy that no longer exists.

As for Hurley, she had to stop her research after she developed a serious allergy to the tree. You win this round, stinging tree.

CHAPTER 2

THE ANTS RUSH OUT

A herd of African elephants tramps across the savanna. In the distance, zebras and antelopes graze.

The hungry elephants approach a cluster of trees. They stuff their mouths with leaves, thorns, and twigs. One elephant wraps its trunk around a thick branch. *Crack!* The branch comes down. Another elephant shoves its body against a tree. *Whuump!* The tree topples over, its roots dangling in the air.

A young elephant wanders away from the group. It approaches another tree. This tree has sharp thorns with round, swollen bases. Each swollen thorn has a mysterious little hole in it.

The elephant doesn't notice the holes. To the youngster, the tree looks delicious.

The elephant wraps its trunk around a branch and tugs. Immediately, small black ants scurry out of the holes. The ants run up the elephant's trunk and reach the sensitive skin around its eyes. The ants bite down with their piercing mandibles and hold fast. More ants swarm into the elephant's trunk and bite the soft, tender skin inside.

The elephant drops the branch in alarm. It shakes its head and wiggles its trunk, trying to dislodge its attackers. It sprints back to the group. It has learned what the other elephants already know: don't mess with that tree.

PLANTS, ANTS, AND ELEPHANTS

An African elephant can weigh up to 14,000 pounds (6,350 kg). It can eat as much as 220 pounds (100 kg) of plant matter in a single day.

With its tremendous strength and huge appetite, an elephant can inflict a lot of damage on a tree. It can rip off thick branches with its trunk. It can topple whole trees. And forget what happens if a herd of elephants comes stomping through.

How does a tree stand a chance?

African trees fight back in different ways. Some grow thick trunks to defend against being bulldozed. Others fill their leaves with poisons. Some trees give up the fight and put their energy into quickly regrowing new branches from broken ones.

But the whistling thorn has a secret weapon: tiny bodyguards. The tree invites stinging ants to move in. The swollen thorns give the ants a place to live.

ATTACKER: *Acacia drepanolobium*

ALIAS: whistling thorn, swollen thorn acacia

ATTACK STRATEGY: guards itself against large, plant-eating animals with stinging ants

KNOWN WHEREABOUTS: savannas of East Africa

Swollen thorns provide a hollow home for biting ants, which defend the tree against attack.

A hungry elephant can do tremendous damage to a tree (left), but the whistling thorn acacia is practically elephant-proof, thanks to its tiny ant bodyguards (right).

Sugary nectar that seeps from the leaves gives the ants food. Four species of African ants fight for the right to live on the tree. The winning ants bite a hole in the thorns and hollow out the inside to build their nests. (The tree gets its name from old, abandoned thorns, which make a whistling sound in the wind.)

The ants get free room and board. In return, they defend the tree, fiercely swarming and biting any intruder.

The whistling thorn grows in the heart of elephant country, yet elephants don't touch it. Ecologists Jacob Goheen and Todd Palmer from Kenya's Mpala Research Centre wondered, Is it possible that tiny ants can drive away the world's largest land animal? Were elephants staying away because the tree tastes bad?

To find out, the two scientists did taste tests on six young elephants being raised at a wildlife center in Kenya. They offered the elephants a choice of food: branches of whistling thorn or branches of another tree known to be a favorite of elephants. None of the branches had ants on them. The young elephants chowed down on both plants. But when the researchers offered the same foods, this time covered with ants, the elephants turned up their long noses.

"What we found is that they like to eat the ant plant as much as their favorite plants—when there are no ants on them," Palmer said.

Next, the scientists asked, Could ant bodyguards really protect whistling thorns from elephants out on the rolling hills of the savanna? To answer this question, the scientists removed ants from some whistling thorn trees. They used smoke to drive the ants away and then put sticky tape around the base of each tree to prevent the ants from returning. They left other whistling thorns alone, with their ants intact. Then they

Todd Palmer from Kenya's Mpala Research Centre studies how ants protect whistling thorns from elephants.

returned after a year to see what had happened. Elephants had munched and battered antless whistling thorns. But whistling thorns that still had their bodyguards remained untouched.

For a tree, the lesson is, when you have to do battle with the world's largest land animal, it's a really good idea to have ants on your side.

CHAPTER 3
A DEADLY SQUEEZE

A hungry fly buzzes through a bog on the trail of something sweet and fruity. It lands on a strange leaf. The leaf is edged with long spines and dripping with sweet nectar. It is the leaf of a Venus flytrap.

The fly begins to slurp the nectar. It brushes against a dark hair on the surface of the leaf. The fly has just alerted the Venus flytrap to its presence. But the fly does not know this. It keeps drinking nectar. It inches forward. It touches another dark hair.

Wham!

The walls of the leaf close in on the fly. The trap has snapped shut. The long spines lock together like the jaws of a hungry animal, and the fly is caught.

The fly frantically tries to free itself. It pushes against the bars of its cage, but the spines do not budge. As the insect struggles, it touches the trigger hairs again and again. This tells the Venus flytrap that it has caught something worthy of its attention. The trap closes tighter. The walls squeeze against the doomed insect.

Acids and digestive juices ooze from the surface of the leaf. The juices trickle into the fly's insides. The insect dissolves into a sloshy broth, and the Venus flytrap laps up its liquid lunch.

After a week, its meal is finished, and the leaf opens again. The Venus flytrap is ready for a fresh victim.

ELECTRIC FLY CATCHER

Many animals eat plants. But this plant bites back: the Venus flytrap catches and eats animals.

The reason for this carnivorous behavior is that the Venus flytrap, like all plants, needs certain nutrients to grow. Plants usually suck these nutrients out of the ground, but the Venus flytrap lives in bogs where the soil is poor. Eating animals gives it a nutrient boost and helps it grow better.

The leaves of the Venus flytrap look like the jaws of a hungry animal. Each leaf is made of two lobes connected by a hinge. Each lobe is edged with a line of sharp spines, called cilia. On the lobes stand a few dark hairs.

To attract prey, the lobes produce nectar and a fruity aroma. When a fly, beetle, or snail crawls across the leaf, the lobes snap shut. Unless the creature is very small, it cannot escape because the cilia lock together like the bars of a cage.

ATTACKER: *Dionaea muscipula*

ALIASES: Venus flytrap, tipitiwitchet

ATTACK STRATEGY: catches and eats insects in a leafy, hair-trigger trap

KNOWN WHEREABOUTS: damp, open pine woodlands in North Carolina and South Carolina

The leaf of a Venus flytrap has two spine-edged lobes connected by a hinge.

The Venus flytrap lures prey with its pink color, fruity smell, and sweet nectar. When an insect shows up—snap!

Then a gland on the inside of the trap releases acids and digestive juices that dissolve the creature.

Scientists have learned that the Venus flytrap feels its prey and senses if the creature is big enough to eat. It accomplishes this feat using those dark hairs that stand on the lobes.

The hairs are the triggers that spring the trap. If one hair is touched, the trap remains open. If two hairs are touched within about twenty seconds, the trap closes.

Why does the trap require two touches? A large insect is likely to touch two hairs in a row. But a single touch could come from almost anything, such as a tiny ant that takes a while to crawl from one hair to another. Or it could be a speck of sand or a falling raindrop.

"The plant does not want to close for a drop of water," said Alexander Volkov of Oakwood University in Alabama.

Volkov has studied how the trap works. He explained that it harnesses something our own nervous systems use: electricity.

Before the trap goes off, the cells of the trap have a negative charge inside and a positive charge outside. When a trigger hair is touched, this electrical charge changes, sending an electrical wave racing across the trap. (Called an action potential, this is the same kind of electrical wave that travels along your nerves.) The wave spreads through the trap's cells. With a second touch of a trigger hair, another wave goes off, and the trap snaps shut.

Volkov and his team wanted to test whether electricity is really causing the trap to close. So they wired a Venus flytrap with tiny electrodes, wires that can carry electricity. They connected one electrode to the hinge and another to a lobe. When they sent a current of electricity through the leaf, the trap closed. They could spring the trap with a zap of electricity.

Volkov's team tested how much electricity was needed to close the trap. They discovered that the amount of charge is a little more than the static electricity you make when you rub two balloons together. This can come as one big wave or as two smaller ones within about twenty seconds. Just like with the trigger hairs. The more the insect struggles and touches the hairs, the more electrical signals go off. In response, the trap squeezes tighter and releases digestive juices.

Dark trigger hairs on each lobe allow the Venus flytrap to sense its prey. With one touch of the trigger hairs, the trap stays open. With a second touch within about twenty seconds of the first, the trap snaps shut.

Is it strange for a plant to use electrical signals? No, said Volkov. "All plants are electrical machines." Most plants use electricity to sense when they are being eaten. But the Venus flytrap has turned the tables, using electricity to catch and devour animals.

CHAPTER 4

SLIPPERY PIT OF DOOM

Deep in the rain forest, a mountain tree shrew scampers through the undergrowth.
It is following an aroma like fruity cabbage. To the tree shrew, the smell means dinner.

The animal enters a clearing. There sits a vase-shaped leaf filled with fluid and topped with a partway-open lid. It is a king pitcher, one of the largest meat-eating plants in the world. Flies buzz back and forth near the plant.

The tree shrew climbs up the side of the pitcher. It straddles the rim, gripping the edges with its four clawed feet. Its body is perched above a half gallon (2 L) of digestive fluid. A few dead flies float in the fluid.

The tree shrew begins to lick nectar from the lid. Its pink tongue flicks in and out. The animal stretches higher to reach more nectar. It rises onto its back legs. As it eats, it drops a pellet of feces—*plip*—right into the pitcher.

The tree shrew hears a faint rustling in the grass. Something is coming. The tree shrew turns, and in that moment, its feet slip.

Splash!

The tree shrew plunges into the pit. It thrashes around in the lethal liquid. It tries to crawl out, but the walls of the pitcher are slippery. Its claws can't get a grip. Soon it stops struggling and drowns.

The unlucky tree shrew (and its feces) will become the king pitcher's next meal.

A TOILET FOR TREE SHREWS

Pitcher plants eat animals to survive. Like the Venus flytrap and other carnivorous plants, pitcher plants grow where the soil is poor. To get the nutrients they need, pitcher plants catch prey in slippery, jug-shaped traps. Scientists call them pit-fall traps.

A pit-fall trap is a devilish device for catching prey. The pitchers attract their prey with sweet nectar, tempting smells, and alluring colors. Insects are their primary targets. When an insect lands, the rim is slick, so the insect easily tumbles in. The walls of the pitcher are slick too, so the poor creature can't get out. It drowns in a mixture of rainwater, acid, and digestive enzymes. Its body dissolves and is absorbed by the walls of the pitcher.

ATTACKER: *Nepenthes rajah*

ALIAS: king pitcher, monkey cup pitcher, giant pitcher

ATTACK STRATEGY: traps and devours insects and small animals in slippery pits, along with a side helping of feces

KNOWN WHEREABOUTS: open, grassy areas in mountain forests on the island of Borneo

A king pitcher catches and traps insects—but small mammals also visit.

Pitcher plants come in many shapes and sizes. They can be shaped like a goblet, a funnel, or a delicate vase. But king pitchers are unusually large—bigger than a football. They are so large that dead tree shrews and drowned rats have been found in them. That made scientists wonder, Is the king pitcher trying to catch and eat mammals?

Charles Clarke of Monash University in Malaysia investigated and found a surprising answer. The king pitcher is not deliberately trapping mammals. The animals fall in while using the pitcher as a toilet.

Clarke and his team found that the mountain tree shrew, *Tupaia montana*, climbs onto the pitcher, straddles the rim, and licks nectar from the lid. As the animal dines, it marks its feeding territory with a dropping of feces. The feces falls right into the pitcher, and the plant digests it. Rich in certain nutrients, the feces supplements the king pitcher's diet of insects.

A pitcher plant dangles like a lantern from the trees.

The king pitcher rests on the ground—a perfect place for a tree shrew toilet.

The plant invites the tree shrew to use it as a toilet. When Clarke's team measured the sizes of lots of different types of pitchers, they found that king pitchers perfectly match the body size of tree shrews. The point of such a large pitcher is that it can catch tree shrew poo. King pitchers also have a curved lid. The lid is shaped like an upside-down bowl with nectar on the inside. There is only one way mountain tree shrews can reach this delicious food.

"They must climb onto the pitchers and orient themselves in such a way that their backsides are located over the pitcher mouths," Clarke said.

Clarke wondered if any other animals used the plant as a toilet. So the team set up video cameras and motion-sensitive cameras in the rain forest to watch the plants after dark. They placed a thin plastic cup inside each pitcher to catch any droppings. They discovered that summit rats (*Rattus baluensis*) arrive at night. The rats too perch on the rim, lick nectar, and deposit their nutrient-rich droppings inside.

The king pitcher's taste for feces helps the hungry plant in its hunt for animal flesh. The foul smell of feces draws flies. If the flies slip into the pit, they too feed the plant. And if a tree shrew or rat should accidentally tumble in—as sometimes happens—the pitcher plant is quite capable of devouring the clumsy, drowned creature.

This summit rat was caught on camera using the king pitcher toilet after dark. The rat leaves behind nutrient-rich feces, which feed the plant and help attract flies.

CHAPTER 5

STINKING DECEPTION

The sun rises over an island where a colony of gulls is nesting. In the pale morning light, gulls wheel in and out, tending their chicks. The doting parents puke up partially digested fish— breakfast for the young ones. The colony is a mess. Bird droppings. Half-eaten fish. Here and there the bodies of dead gulls. The place is buzzing with flies.

In this messy scene, a dead horse arum is blooming. The hairy blossom has a dark, blood-colored outer wrapping that looks like a dead animal. The wrapping forms a chamber, with tiny flowers hidden inside. Sticking out of the entrance to the chamber is a hairy, tail-like thing.

As the sun rises, a female blowfly crawls out of the chamber. Her hairy body is dusted with yellow pollen. The fly buzzes around, looking for a place to lay her eggs, perhaps the body of a dead gull. Rotting meat is perfect food for her maggots.

Nearby, a second dead horse arum bursts into bloom. The dark, meat-colored blossom reeks like a dead animal. Soon the fly is buzzing toward the stinky plant. To the female fly, the dead horse arum seems like a perfect spot to lay her eggs. Thinking she has found a corpse, she looks for a hole to enter the body. She crawls along the tail-like thing, into the chamber.

The inside of the chamber is dark and warm and foul smelling—just like the inside of a rotting corpse. Fooled, the female fly begins to lay her eggs. But the maggots that hatch from those eggs will die. There is no food for them here.

The fly turns to leave, but she cannot escape. A row of spines is blocking her way. She tries to climb over the spines, but she falls back to the bottom of the chamber.

She is trapped.

LORD OF THE FLIES

The dead horse arum is famous for its ability to mimic a dead animal.

In bloom, the plant makes a spathe, a leaf that is about as wide as a dinner plate. The spathe is a blotchy, purplish color. It looks just like a hunk of meat. The spathe wraps around a hairy spike, called an appendix, which looks like a tail.

ATTACKER: *Helicodiceros muscivorus*

ALIAS: dead horse arum, dragon's mouth, pig butt arum, carrion flower, corpse flower

ATTACK STRATEGY: kidnaps blowflies for pollination

KNOWN WHEREABOUTS: seashores and seabird colonies on islands of the Mediterranean

With its color, smell, and heat, a dead horse arum mimics a rotting carcass.

The reason for the plant's gruesome appearance? Reproduction. The spathe forms a chamber. Inside the chamber are tiny male and female flowers. In order for the dead horse arum to make seeds, pollen—the male sex cell—must move from a male flower of one dead horse arum to a female flower of a different dead horse arum. But pollen can't move on its own, so the plant lures helpers. Other plants use bright colors and sweet nectar to entice helpers such as bees or butterflies. The dead horse arum draws flies by mimicking a corpse.

The blossom releases a disgusting smell, like a rotting carcass. It even produces its own heat, just as decomposing flesh does. The warmth helps launch that nasty stench into the air.

If the plant can fool a carrion-loving blowfly into entering the chamber, the fly's body will pick up pollen. If the fly then brings that pollen to the chamber of another dead horse arum, the

Reeking like rotten flesh, a dead horse arum lures a fly by imitating a corpse. The plant's goal is to trick the fly into crawling into the chamber and picking up pollen.

A fly that enters the dead horse arum's chamber will become the plant's prisoner.

female flowers on the new plant will get pollinated. But for the pollination scheme to work, the plant must kidnap the fly and hold it hostage.

The scheme begins as a female fly crawls out of one dead horse arum, its body coated with pollen that it picked up inside. The fly buzzes to a new dead horse arum. This new blossom is warm and foul smelling. Fooled by the warmth and the smell, the fly lands on the tail-like appendix. She follows the appendix and enters the chamber.

In the darkness, the fly passes by a band of tiny male flowers. The male flowers are not yet producing pollen. The fly pushes onward, scrambling over a row of spines. Then she passes the tiny female flowers. Finally, she reaches the bottom and lays her eggs. The eggs are doomed, though.

Dead Horse Arum Pollination

DAY

STEP 1 — A blowfly crawls out of a dead horse arum. Its body is dusted with pollen.

PLANT 1 — appendix, spath

STEP 2 — Another dead horse arum blooms, producing warmth and a foul odor. Inside the chamber, female flowers are ready to be pollinated. The male flowers are not yet ripe.

PLANT 2

STEP 3 — The fly enters the chamber of the new dead horse arum.

male flowers, spines, female flowers, floral chamber

STEP 4 — The fly travels through the spines to the chamber bottom where it lays its eggs.

pollen-covered blowfly, blowfly eggs

STEP 5 — Spines block the exit. As the fly tries to escape, it brushes against the female flowers. The pollen (from PLANT 1) from its body rubs off on them.

trapped blowfly

NIGHT

STEP 6 — During the night, pollen erupts from the male flowers. The spines that are blocking the exit shrivel. The fly is free to leave.

ripened male flowers covered with pollen, shriveled spines

STEP 7 — On the way out of the chamber, the fly climbs over the male flowers, picking up their pollen.

pollen-covered blowfly

STEP 8 — With its fresh load of pollen (from PLANT 2), the fly arrives at a new dead horse arum that has just bloomed. It enters the chamber and pollinates the female flowers.

PLANT 3

When the fly turns to leave, she finds she is trapped by the spines. As she crawls around trying to get out, pollen from her body brushes onto the female flowers. These flowers can now make seeds. But the plant isn't finished with the fly.

During the night, with the fly trapped inside, the male flowers ripen. Sticky yellow pollen bursts out. Then the spines that block the exit shrivel.

As morning dawns, the fly is free to go. On her way out, she must climb over the male flowers. Her bristly body picks up a fresh load of pollen.

The fly leaves and does not return. The flower is no longer warm. It no longer makes its foul perfume. The illusion has ended, and the fly loses interest. She takes her load of pollen and heads elsewhere.

With any luck, she will fall for the trick again and carry her load of pollen to the next dead horse arum in her path.

Fooled by the plant's imitation of a rotting corpse, flies swarm to a dead horse arum.

CHAPTER 6
THE BIRD CATCHER

From its nest in a tree, a lesser noddy looks around. The young gray bird is ready to fly. It does not know that danger lurks in these branches.

This is a pisonia tree. It grows on tropical beaches. People call it the bird-catcher tree.

The tree is dangerous because of its seeds—and this pisonia tree is full of them. The seeds dangle in clusters from the limbs. They form tangled piles on the ground. Pisonia seeds are sticky and covered with hooks. They stick to almost anything that brushes against them.

The lesser noddy hops out of the nest onto the branch. It looks down. It does not notice the pile of bird bones at the base of the tree. Carefully, the noddy inches along the branch. It stretches its wings. A cluster of seeds sticks to one wing like glue.

The noddy flaps to the ground. It takes a few hops. It brushes against a pile of seeds. More seeds cling to its other wing.

The young bird flaps its wings to try to free itself. It tries to pry the seeds loose with its long beak. But the seeds are too sticky.

Weighed down and unable to fly, it wanders along the beach. If its parents don't find it, it will drown in the surf. And that's only if hungry beach crabs don't get it first.

THE MYSTERY OF THE MURDEROUS SEEDS

Pisonia trees don't look dangerous. If you saw one growing on a warm tropical island, you might think it was a typical tree. Until you notice the bones.

Pisonia seeds hitchhike on birds. The seeds are covered with tiny hooks and coated with a sticky glue. Many birds become so entangled they die. Some pisonia trees have a pile of sun-bleached bones at their roots. Or a dead bird dangling from their branches. Alan Burger wanted to know why.

Burger is a seabird biologist at the University of Victoria in Canada. He came to Cousin Island in the Indian Ocean to study birds. While walking along the beach, he noticed dead birds covered with pisonia seeds.

It's not unusual for seeds to hook themselves onto an animal. Many seeds travel this way. (If you've ever plucked burrs from your socks, you know this firsthand.) But it is truly bizarre for a seed to *kill* the animal that gives it a ride. What was the tree's motive?

ATTACKER: *Pisonia grandis*

ALIASES: grand devil's claws, bird-catcher tree, bird-eater tree, birdlime tree, Mapou tree

ATTACK STRATEGY: glues its seeds onto seabirds, entangling them and leading to the bird's death

KNOWN WHEREABOUTS: along the coast and shoreline of coral islands in the Indian and Pacific Oceans

The bird-catcher tree grows on tropical beaches that are teeming with birds.

If this entangled noddy is able to fly, it may spread pisonia seeds to another island.

Some scientists thought pisonia killed birds for the nutrients. Their hypothesis was that seeds that sprouted beside a rotting bird carcass would get a dose of fertilizer to help them grow. But no one had tested the fertilizer hypothesis.

So Burger collected dead seabirds covered with pisonia seeds. He counted the seeds, placed the seedy carcasses on the ground, and kept track of how many seeds grew. For comparison, he scattered seeds on the ground and counted how many of these grew.

Did seeds stuck to a carcass grow better? No. They grew worse. The reason is that seabird carcasses make a good meal. "The crabs eat them," Burger said. "There's lots of cockroaches that eat them. So within a couple of weeks, that carcass is eaten up." He realized that the fertilizer hypothesis is wrong.

Then Burger investigated what would happen if a dead, entangled bird washed out to sea. Maybe the carcass acted like a raft and carried the seeds to another island where they could grow.

To test this, he soaked pisonia seeds in seawater for long periods. He wanted to simulate what would happen if seeds were stuck to a floating carcass. But the soaked seeds didn't survive long. After just twelve days, none of the seeds sprouted. So the floating raft idea didn't seem right either.

Finally, he tested whether the seeds might reach an island on a living bird. Birds with only a few seeds stuck to them can still fly. Tropical seabirds don't rest on the water, but they do snatch fish from the waves. So Burger dipped the seeds in seawater for just thirty minutes a day. After a month, many of the seeds still sprouted.

"That seems to be the logical way in which the seeds are going to get from one island to another," said Burger. "By being attached to a live seabird rather than a dead seabird."

It seems the tree kills birds by accident. Only a living bird can bring the seed to another island. From the viewpoint of the tree, as long as enough birds survive to carry its seeds, the hitchhiking is a success.

Despite the dangers, lesser noddies nest in pisonia trees in great numbers.

CHAPTER 7

ATTACK OF THE VAMPIRE VINE

On a summer night, the sun sets on a freshly dug garden. Darkness descends. A raccoon creeps through the shadows. An owl peers down from a tree.

Out of the newly dug ground, a wiry vine rises. The vine is orange, not green like most plants. It is called dodder. It doesn't have roots or even leaves. It doesn't need them.

The vine has one goal: find food. Rising in the blackness, the vine wiggles about. It sweeps round and round in slow circles. It is searching the way you might with your hands in front of you when you're blindfolded.

As the vine bends and sweeps and grows, it sniffs the air. It smells a tomato plant growing nearby. The vine changes its direction of growth. It twists and bends, moving toward the smell.

Closer. Closer. Almost there.

At last, it bumps into a leaf of the tomato plant. The vine drops to the ground. It gropes along the ground until it finds the tomato's stem. The vine grabs on, winding around and around the stem. Tiny knobs sink like fangs into the tomato plant's stem. The dodder vine begins to suck out its host's juices. Fed by these vital fluids, the vine grows stronger.

Over the days and nights of summer, the dodder vine shoots out more tentacles. These wind around and around its host. Soon the tomato looks as if it has been attacked with orange silly string. As the vampire vine thrives, its host grows weaker and weaker.

A SAP-SUCKING PARASITE

Dodder is a strange plant. This orange vine belongs to a group of more than one hundred closely related plants, all yellow, orange, or white. Most have no leaves or roots but, instead, are a tangle of stems. You might mistake one for a pile of spaghetti.

Dodder is a parasite. Parasites feed off other living things. Dodder feeds off a host plant's sap, the sugar-filled fluid that flows through the plant's veins. Dodder reaches this rich food by using strangling tendrils that wrap around a host plant's stem. It pierces the stem with toothlike knobs and sucks out the sap.

ATTACKER: *Cuscuta* spp.

ALIAS: strangleweed, devil's-gut, witches' shoelaces, love vine, hell weed, witches' hair

ATTACK STRATEGY: sucks the juices from other plants

KNOWN WHEREABOUTS: sunny or partly shady ground on every continent except Antarctica

Dodder vines survive by winding around a host plant and sucking out its juices.

Why does dodder behave this way? "In order to survive they must attach to a host plant," said plant biologist Consuelo De Moraes. "They work like vampires in a sense."

Dodder cannot make its own food from sunlight. It has no chlorophyll, the green pigment that plants use to carry out photosynthesis. A young dodder plant's only chance of surviving is to find a host plant and feed on it. A new dodder seedling has only a few days to find food before it dies.

De Moraes and her team at Penn State University wondered how dodder finds a host plant. So they put dodder to the test. First, they put a dodder vine next to a potted tomato plant. The vine leaned toward the tomato plant. Then they placed the vine next to a pot with soil but no plant. The vine didn't do anything. The dodder vine was clearly sensing the tomato plant.

Dodder vines may be orange, yellow, or white—but never green. This strange plant is a tangle of stems with no leaves.

Next, the scientists tested whether dodder could see the plant. So they placed a dodder vine next to a fake plant made from pipe cleaners and felt. The vine wasn't fooled. They placed the vine beside vials of green- or red-colored water. Still no reaction.

But every time they put a dodder next to a real tomato plant, the dodder went for it. It didn't matter if the tomato plant was well lit, in the dark, or hidden behind an object. The vine knew the tomato plant was there.

The team had a hunch dodder was *smelling* its host. After all, all plants give off odors. As they grow, they release water vapor into the air along with a blend of chemicals. You can think of this blend as a plant's perfume.

Was dodder smelling the tomato's perfume? To test this, the scientists extracted scent chemicals from the tomato plant and dabbed them on a piece of rubber. When they placed a dodder next to the scented rubber, the dodder leaned toward the scent. They then put a dodder in one closed box and a tomato plant in another closed box. They connected the boxes with a hose that let air blow between the boxes. The dodder leaned toward the tube opening. It could smell the tomato-scented air wafting in from the tube.

The team learned that dodder is a finicky eater. If placed near two plants, a dodder could identify which plants they were and grow toward the one it prefers. Given a choice of tomato or wheat, the vampire vine chose a juicy tomato plant every time.

THE DODDER EXPERIMENTS

SIGHT 1 — dodder vine D — real tomato plant T
The vine grew toward the real tomato plant.

SIGHT 2 — D — only soil in the pot S
The vine didn't grow toward the soil.

SIGHT 3 — D — fake tomato plant F
The vine didn't grow toward the fake plant.

SIGHT 4 — D — vials of colored water
The vine didn't grow toward the water vials.

SCENT 5 — D — TOMATO PLANT IN THE DARK
The vine grew toward the darkened plant.

SCENT 6 — OBSTRUCTION — D — T
The vine grew toward the obstructed plant.

SCENT 7 — scent chemicals extracted from tomato plant → scent chemicals applied to rubber — dodder vine D
The vine grew toward a piece of rubber smeared with tomato scent chemicals.

SCENT 8 — ↑ THIS END UP ↑ — D — hose — ↑ THIS END UP ↑ — T
The vine grew toward the real tomato plant, even when both were enclosed in boxes.

SCENT 9 — real tomato plant T — dodder vine D — wheat plant W
The vine showed preference for the real tomato plant over the wheat plant.

CHAPTER 8

CREEPING, CLIMBING INVADER

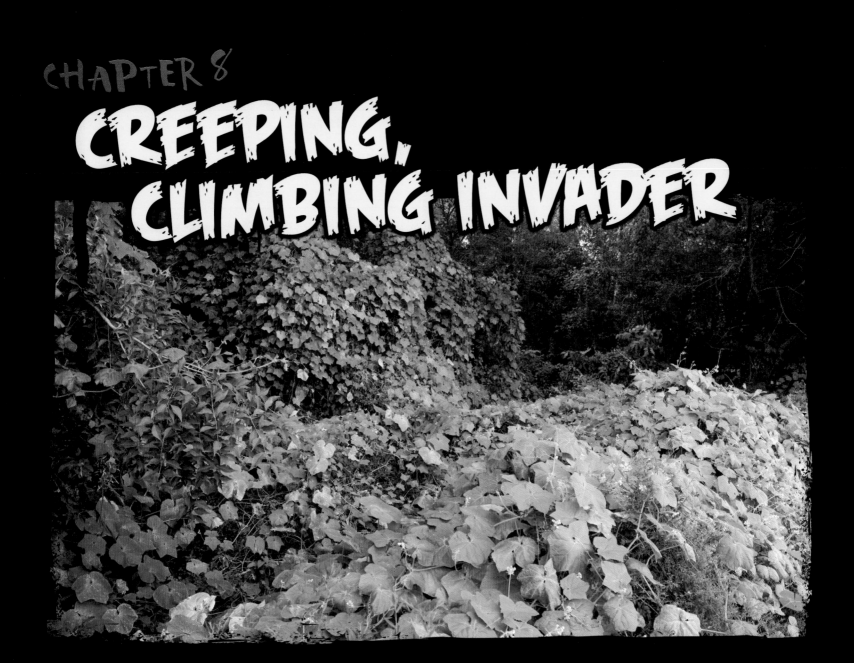

The spring sun rises on a small house in the woods. The rooms inside are dark because the owners have gone away. A toad hops across the abandoned porch. A robin builds its nest under the porch roof.

Out of the woods creeps a kudzu vine. The ropelike vine grows quickly in the warm spring air. Its leaves twist and swivel, boosting the amount of sunlight they receive. In a few days, the vine reaches the porch steps. In a week, it has slithered onto the porch. It begins to shimmy up the porch posts, heading for the roof.

Meanwhile, more kudzu vines emerge from the forest. Snakelike, the vines creep and crawl toward the house. Every so often, they sink new roots into the ground. From these roots, more vines shoot out, a vast web of them creeping forward.

Soon they too reach the little house. One vine wraps itself around the mailbox. Another winds around the downspout. More vines creep up the back door and press against the windows.

When autumn comes, the owners return. They can barely see their home under the tangle of vines and leaves. Their house has been swallowed by kudzu.

THE VINE THAT ATE THE SOUTH

Kudzu (KUD-zoo) is one of America's most hated weeds, but that wasn't always the case. It first came to the country in 1876 for the Philadelphia Centennial Exposition. Countries were invited to set up exhibits in honor of the one hundredth birthday of the United States. The Japanese government created a beautiful garden featuring kudzu. Gardeners were impressed with its pretty purple flowers that smelled like grapes. They loved the way the vine could quickly drape a porch in lush, leafy shade.

Americans went crazy for kudzu. In the first half of the twentieth century, they bought millions of plants. They joined kudzu clubs. They held kudzu-planting contests. They threw kudzu festivals.

To farmers, kudzu seemed like a miracle plant. They could feed it to their animals. And kudzu gripped the soil and prevented erosion. The government paid farmers to plant it and hired workers to plant kudzu along roadways.

And all those kudzu plants grew and grew and grew.

ATTACKER: *Pueraria* spp.

ALIASES: kudzu, mile-a-minute, vine that ate the South, drop it and run vine

ATTACK STRATEGY: grows over structures and smothers other plants, starving them of sunlight

KNOWN WHEREABOUTS: roadsides, forest edges, abandoned fields, and vacant lots in North America; native to China, Taiwan, Japan, and India

Kudzu's grape-scented flowers once charmed gardeners—but the plant is a killer.

And then people discovered something about kudzu: there was almost no way to stop it.

In the hot, humid summers of the southern United States, the vine can grow 1 foot (30 cm) a day. In a week, it can climb over the head of a full-grown man. In a single summer, it can scramble to the top of the tallest tree. Wherever the vine touches the ground, it can sink new roots, which can then shoot out more vines. Just one of its carrot-shaped roots can grow to weigh 400 pounds (181 kg).

Kudzu's tangled mats of ropy vines and big green leaves overwhelm other plants. Its thick vegetation won't let any light through to the plants trying to grow underneath. Which means that when kudzu takes over, soon the only thing left alive is . . . kudzu.

Kudzu took hold of the South and wouldn't let go. It smothered buildings. It devoured cars. It strangled young trees and toppled old ones. It pulled down power lines. It crept across railroad tracks, causing trains to jump the tracks.

Kudzu smothers a building in Georgia.

Some people said if you listened hard enough, you could hear it growing. People nervously joked about closing the windows at night to keep it out of the house.

What really makes kudzu so deadly is that it doesn't belong in North America. Scientists call it an invasive species. The vine comes from eastern Asia, where it lives and grows alongside natural diseases and predators. In its native habitat, many insects feast on kudzu and keep it from spreading, so it doesn't become a pest. But none of its natural enemies lives in North America, and that gives kudzu an unfair advantage. While North American plants are getting munched by native insects, kudzu has no enemies to stop its growth.

In Maryland a herd of hungry goats devours the last of a patch of kudzu.

And so kudzu grows and grows and grows.

By one estimate, the vine has swallowed 7 million acres (2.8 million ha) of the South—an area the size of Massachusetts.

But people are fighting back. Their secret weapon? Goats! The animals love to munch the stuff. A herd of goats can get a patch of kudzu under control. But goats aren't the only ones that find kudzu worth eating. Some people in the South figure, if you can't beat kudzu, you can at least chow down on it. People eat kudzu leaves raw, boiled, or deep fried. The flowers make tasty jelly.

Just remember to close the windows at night.

THE QUEST FOR SURVIVAL

Why do plants go out of their way to do harm? Why do they kidnap, murder, and invade?

Plants aren't sinister. They have no brains. Plants such as the stinging tree, *Dendrocnide moroides*, don't *decide* to sting their enemies. So why do they do it?

Like animals, plants are on a quest to survive. Plants need water, light, and a few nutrients. They must also struggle to fight off their enemies. If a change in a behavior or body part helps a plant survive, that plant may be able to make more offspring. If the offspring inherit that change, the species can evolve, or change over time.

Look at the stinging tree. The plant uses poison-filled hairs to defend itself against hungry animals. If the plant can avoid becoming someone's lunch, it can improve its odds of making seeds. Over many years, plants with poison-filled hairs may become more common than closely related plants that don't have this defense.

Given enough time, this relationship between a plant and its enemy can lead to a sort of arms race. The plant develops a poison to keep away something that is eating it. And so the plant eater changes over time to tolerate the poison. Then the plant fights back by making a more powerful poison. In response, the animal evolves greater tolerance . . . and so on.

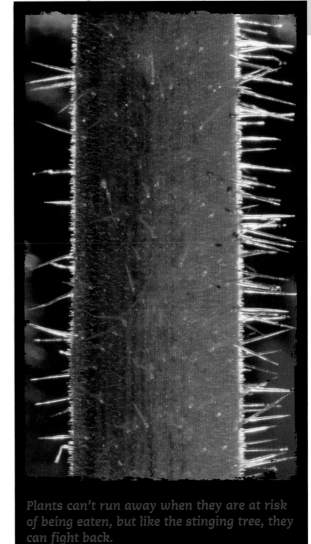

Plants can't run away when they are at risk of being eaten, but like the stinging tree, they can fight back.

Is that how the stinging tree got its sting? The answer is a mystery. It is one of many unsolved mysteries from the dark side of the plant world. Solving these stories will require brave people willing to tramp into the wild and spend time with fascinating, dangerous plants—people who have curiosity, a taste for adventure, and a dedication to the natural world. Maybe a person like you.

But tread carefully. The plants are waiting for you, and they are ready to attack.

AUTHOR'S NOTE

Charles Darwin called Venus flytrap "one of the most wonderful plants in the world." I think all the plants in this book are wonderful. What I love about them is the way they turn our ideas about plants upside down. Most of us think of plants as harmless, passive, and unable to move. But the ones in this book are skilled, cunning survivors.

If you are fascinated by the plants in this book, you might discover that a botanical garden near you has some weird plants on display. You can go there and see them up close for yourself. But if you really want to get to know plants, try getting your hands on an ordinary packet of seeds. You can learn a lot by growing plants yourself.

Some people are so fascinated by plants that they collect them from the wild and bring them home. Please do not do this! Some of the species in this book, such as the Venus flytrap, are endangered (at risk of disappearing forever). When people collect specimens from the wild, those plants are gone. If you want to grow a Venus flytrap or other carnivorous plants, you'll find lists of reputable dealers and loads of growing information from the International Carnivorous Plant Society (www.carnivorousplants.org).

When I was writing this book, a number of scientists kindly took time from their busy schedules to share their experiences, answer my questions, and explain difficult concepts to me. I would like to thank Dr. Alan Burger at the University of Victoria in Canada; Dr. Rainer Hedrich, Dr. Ines Kreuzer, and Dr. Sönke Scherzer at the University of Würzburg in Germany; Dr. Marina Hurley at the University of New South Wales in Australia; and Dr. Alexander Volkov at Oakwood University in Alabama. These men and women have worked hard to expand our understanding of the world's weirdest plants. I am grateful for the opportunity to share their discoveries with you.

SOURCE NOTES

5   Buel, J. W. *Sea and Land: An Illustrated History of the Wonderful and Curious Things of Nature Existing Before and Since the Deluge.* Philadelphia: Historical Publishing, 1889.

7   Amanda Burdon, "Gympie Gympie: Once Stung, Never Forgotten," *Australian Geographic*, June 16, 2009, http://www.australiangeographic.com.au/topics/science-environment/2009/06/gympie-gympie-once-stung,-never-forgotten.

8–9   Marina Hurley, "Selective Stingers," *ECOS* 105 (October 2000): 18–23.

9   Marina Hurley, personal communication with author, December 19, 2017.

13   Sindya N. Bhanoo, "In a Fight for a Tree, Ants Thwart Elephants," *New York Times*, September 6, 2010, http://www.nytimes.com/2010/09/07/science/07obants.html.

16   Alexander Volkov, Skype interview with author, October 13, 2017.

17   Volkov.

21   Matt Walker, "Giant Meat-Eating Plants Prefer to Eat Tree Shrew Poo," *Earth News*, last modified March 10, 2010, http://news.bbc.co.uk/earth/hi/earth_news/newsid_8552000/8552157.stm.

30   Alan Burger, personal communication with author, October 31, 2017.

31   Burger.

34   *Through the Wormhole*, season 4, episode 4, "How Do Aliens Think?," directed by David LaMattina, written by Kurt Sayenga, featuring Morgan Freeman, aired June 19, 2013, on the Science Channel, https://www.imdb.com/title/tt3000288/?ref_=ttep_ep4.

42   Oxford University Press, "No Such Thing as a Free Lunch for Venus Flytraps," *ScienceDaily*, August 3, 2010, https://www.sciencedaily.com/releases/2010/08/100803101922.htm.

GLOSSARY

acid: a chemical compound that can burn skin

carcass: the dead body of an animal

carnivorous: feeding on animal flesh

carrion: dead and decaying flesh

chlorophyll: the green-colored chemical found in plants and needed to carry out photosynthesis

colony: a group of animals that belong to one species, living and breeding together in a particular place

corpse: the dead body of an animal

decomposing: breaking down the chemicals in a living thing; rotting

ecologist: a person who studies the relationships between living things and their environment

electrodes: devices used to send an electric current through a living tissue, such as a plant leaf

enzymes: complex proteins made by living cells that perform or speed up reactions, such as the digestion of food

erosion: the wearing away of soil by water or wind

evolve: to develop by a series of gradual changes

feces: solid or semisolid animal waste; also called animal droppings, excrement, or poop

gland: a layer of plant cells that makes and discharges a substance for use in the body of the plant

herbivores: animals that eat plants

host: a living plant or animal that has a parasite living on or in it

hypothesis: an untested idea to explain an observation that can be tested by further study or investigation

invasive species: a plant, animal, or fungus species that is not native to a location and becomes a nuisance, often causing damage to native species

invertebrates: animals that lack backbones, such as worms, snails, spiders, or insects

lethal: capable of causing death

lobes: curved or rounded parts of a plant leaf

maggot: a soft, wormlike larva of a fly

mammals: a class of vertebrates that nourish their young with milk and have hair on their bodies

mandibles: the jaws of an insect or other invertebrate used for biting

native: living or growing naturally in a particular place

nectar: a sweet liquid produced by plants to lure animals

nerves: stringy bands of tissue that connect the brain and spinal cord with other parts of the body

parasite: a living thing that lives in or on another living thing, called the host, and that benefits from living this way while the host is harmed

photosynthesis: the process by which plants use chlorophyll to make carbohydrates from water and carbon dioxide in the air in the presence of light

pollen: tiny particles made by flowers that fertilize the seeds

pollinated: transferred pollen from the male to the female part of a flower

predator: an animal that eats other animals for food

preen: to smooth or clean feathers with the beak or bill, as birds do

prey: an animal eaten by a predator

reproduce: to make new individuals of the same kind

sap: the juice that circulates through a plant and carries water and food

savanna: a grassland with scattered trees spaced widely apart

seabird: a bird that lives in or on the open ocean, such as a gull or albatross

silica: a chemical compound that is a component of quartz and sand. Silica sand is used to make glass.

species: a particular type of living thing

toxin: a poison

tree shrew: a kind of small mammal found in Southeast Asia, resembling a squirrel and having a long snout

SELECTED BIBLIOGRAPHY

You can find the complete bibliography of sources consulted at http://rebeccahirsch.com/when-plants-attack.html.

Attenborough, David. *The Private Life of Plants: A Natural History of Plant Behaviour*. Princeton: Princeton University Press, 1995.

Blaustein, Richard J. "Kudzu's Invasion into Southern United States Life and Culture." In *The Great Reshuffling: Human Dimensions of Invasive Species*, edited by J. A. McNeely, 55–62. Gland, Switzerland, and Cambridge, UK: World Conservation Union, 2001.

Burger, Alan E. "Dispersal and Germination of Seeds of *Pisonia grandis*, an Indo-Pacific Tropical Tree Associated with Insular Seabird Colonies." *Journal of Tropical Ecology* 21, no. 3 (May 2005): 263–271.

Chamovitz, Daniel. *What a Plant Knows: A Field Guide to the Senses*. New York: Farrar, Straus and Giroux, 2012.

Chin, Lijin, Jonathan A. Moran, and Charles Clarke. "Trap Geometry in Three Giant Montane Pitcher Plant Species from Borneo Is a Function of Tree Shrew Body Size." *New Phytologist* 186, no. 2 (April 2010): 461–470.

Goheen, Jacob R., and Todd M. Palmer. "Defensive Plant-Ants Stabilize Megaherbivore-Driven Landscape Change in an African Savanna." *Current Biology* 20, no. 19 (October 2010): 1768–1772.

Hurley, Marina. "Selective Stingers." *Ecos* 105 (October 1, 2000): 18–23.

Runyon, Justin B., Mark C. Meschler, and Consuelo M. De Moraes. "Volatile Chemical Cues Guide Host Location and Host Selection by *Parasitic Plants*." *Science* 313, no. 5795 (September 29, 2006): 1964–1967.

Stensmyr, Marcus C., Isabella Urru, Ignazio Collu, Malin Celander, Bill S. Hansson, and Anna-Maria Angioy. "Rotting Smell of Dead-Horse Arum Florets." *Nature* 420 (December 12, 2002): 625–626.

Volkov, Alexander G., Monique-Reneé Pinnock, Dennell C. Lowe, Ma'Resha S. Gay, and Vladislav S. Martin. "Complete Hunting Cycle of *Dionaea muscipula*: Consecutive Steps and Their Electrical Properties." *Journal of Plant Physiology* 168, no. 2 (January 2011): 109–120.

MORE TO EXPLORE

Books

Blevins, Wiley. *Ninja Plants: Survival and Adaptation in the Plant World*. Minneapolis: Twenty-First Century Books, 2017. Discover more about the sneaky and deceitful ways of plants. In these pages, you'll find plants that eat meat, repel with a horrible smell, poison their victims, and manage to survive in extreme conditions.

Johnson, Rebecca L. *When Lunch Fights Back: Wickedly Clever Animal Defenses*. Minneapolis: Millbrook Press, 2015. Can't get enough bizarre stories of living things? Check out the ways some animals and plants defend themselves from attack.

Stewart, Amy. *Wicked Plants: The Weed That Killed Lincoln's Mother and Other Botanical Atrocities*. New York: Algonquin Books, 2009. This book is chock full of stories of treacherous, deceptive, and poisonous plants.

Willis, Kathy. *Botanicum: Welcome to the Museum*. Somerville, MA: Big Picture, 2017. Want to learn more about the world of plants? In this book you can see and read about beautiful, exotic, and weird plants of the world and how they work.

Websites and Videos

"Dead Horse Arum"
https://www.youtube.com/watch?v=OelTxxW0GvY
Watch up close how a dead horse arum lures flies by mimicking a corpse.

"Dr Marina Hurley and Her Stinging Tree Research"
https://www.youtube.com/watch?v=2VS69FXbjN8
This video takes you into the Australian rain forest with Dr. Marina Hurley to visit stinging trees.

Invasive and Problem Plants of the United States
http://thewildclassroom.com/biodiversity/problemplants/
Learn more about kudzu and other invasive and problem plants in the US.

"Kudzu—a Very Wicked Plant"
https://www.youtube.com/watch?v=0-Hbl0bV8FA
Wander into a patch of kudzu in this short video.

"Poisonous Pitcher Plant"
https://www.youtube.com/watch?v=trWzDlRvv1M
Get up close with carnivorous pitcher plants and watch a time-lapse video of how a leaf inflates to form a beautiful but deadly pitcher.

Tomato and Dodder Plant
http://news.psu.edu/video/223466/2011/06/10/tomato-and-dodder-plant
This brief video clip shows dodder sensing and attacking a tomato plant.

"Tree Shrew on *Nepenthes rajah*"
https://www.youtube.com/watch?v=wUMg6CGInM8
Watch this short video to see a mountain tree shrew visiting a king pitcher plant.

When Plants Attack: A Time-Lapse
https://www.theatlantic.com/video/index/383907/when-plants-attack-a-time-lapse/
This eerie time-lapse video shows the ways pitcher plants, Venus flytraps, and other carnivorous plants eat insects.

Wicked Plants
http://www.untamedscience.com/blog/wicked-plants/
Meet ten murderous members of the plant kingdom with facts, photos, and videos.

INDEX

PHOTO ACKNOWLEDGMENTS

Image credits: Design: Bipsun/Shutterstock.com; alanadesign/Shutterstock.com shekaka/Shutterstock.com; nicemonkey/Shutterstock.com; Husjak/Shutterstock.com. Content: © Unno Kazuo/Minden Pictures, p. 1; Mayur Kotlikar/Moment Open/Getty Images, pp. 2–3; 16, 42, 43, 44, 45, 46, 47, 48; Robsonphoto/Shutterstock.com, p. 4; Wikimedia Commons (public domain), p. 5; © Jurgen Freund/Minden Pictures, pp. 6, 7, 8; Courtesy of Marina Hurley, p. 9; Roger de la Harpe/Education Images/UIG/Getty Images, pp. 10–11; Paul Davies/Alamy Stock Photo, p. 12 (left); Premaphotos/Alamy Stock Photo, p. 12 (right); Courtesy Todd Palmer, p. 13; hiriet/Andia.fr/Getty Images, p. 14; Ed Reschke/Photolibrary/Getty Images, p. 15; monica-photo/iStock/Getty Images, p. 17; Ch'ien Lee/Minden Pictures/Getty Images, pp. 18, 20 (right), 21; RGB Ventures/SuperStock/Alamy Stock Photo, p. 19; EyeEm/Getty Images, p. 20 (left); © Miles Barton/NPL/Minden Pictures, p. 22; Natural Visions/Alamy Stock Photo, p. 23; Mike Read/Alamy Stock Photo, p. 24; Nature's Images/Science Source/Getty Images, p. 25; Laura Westlund/Independent Picture Service, pp. 26, 35; Mike Read/Alamy Stock Photo, p. 27; © Peter Reynolds/Minden Pictures, p. 28; DEA/P. JACCOD/Getty Images, p. 29; Kevin Schafer/Minden Pictures/Getty Images, p. 30; © Peter Reynolds/Minden Pictures, p. 31; Stuart Wilson/Science Source/Getty Images, p. 32; Nature Photographers Ltd/Alamy Stock Photo, p. 33; Werner Bollmann/Oxford Scientific/Getty Images, p. 34; Miguel Megevand/Getty Images, p. 36; Matt Meadows/Photolibrary/Getty Images, p. 37; Grant Heilman Photography/Alamy Stock Photo, p. 38; Michael S. Williamson/The Washington Post/Getty Images, p. 39; blickwinkel/Alamy Stock Photo, pp. 40–41; © Jurgen Freund/NPL/Minden Pictures, p. 41.

Front cover: blickwinkel/Alamy Stock Photo. Back cover: Mayur Kotlikar/Moment Open/Getty Images. Jacket flaps: Roger de la Harpe/Education Images/UIG/Getty Images.